HAIKU *Love*

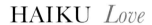

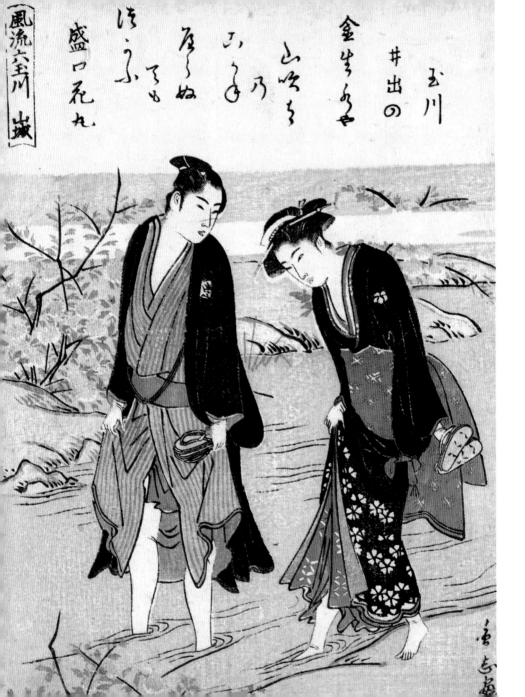

HAIKU

Love

Edited by
Alan Cummings

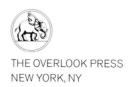

THE OVERLOOK PRESS
NEW YORK, NY

To Keiko

First published in the
United States in 2013 by
The Overlook Press,
Peter Mayer Publishers, Inc.
141 Wooster Street
New York, NY 10012
www.overlookpress.com

For bulk and special sales please
contact sales@overlookny.com

ISBN 978-4683-0860-0

First published in the
United Kingdom in 2013 by
The British Museum Press

Alan Cummings has asserted
the right to be identified as the
author of this work.

Designed by Jade Design

Printed in China by 1010
Printing International Ltd

Frontispiece Angyūsai Enshi
(active 1770s–1790s), *Yamashiro*
from the series *Fashionable
Six Jewel Rivers* (*Furyu Mu-
Tamagawa*). Color woodblock
print, 1780s. 22 x 15.4 cm.
British Museum 1907,0531,0.451.

Contents

Introduction

Haiku

Haiku are the most internationally recognizable of Japanese poetic forms: short, seventeen-syllable poems arranged in the form 5-7-5, they usually focus on the seasons or the natural world and include an identifiable seasonal word (*kigo*). They became the most popular form of Japanese poetry in the late seventeenth century (though the term haiku itself didn't come into use until the late nineteenth century), and it is estimated that today there may be as many as five million practitioners (*haijin*) in Japan. But for much of Japanese history, it was not haiku but *tanka* that was the most important and respected poetic form. *Tanka* are thirty-one syllable poems, arranged in the pattern 5-7-5-7-7. They were particularly important at the imperial court from the Heian period (794–1185) onwards, where poetry functioned as a kind of social and cultural 'glue'[1]. *Tanka* had both a public and a private face: they were used as a means of courtship between lovers and communication between relatives and friends; their composition and recitation marked many formal court events, and for a poet to succeed in publishing a verse in one of the official imperial anthologies, it was a signal of honour indeed.

The sharp-eyed reader may have noticed that the first three 'lines' (Japanese poems are traditionally written in one line, but English translations usually treat the 5-7-5-7-7 structure as five separate lines) of a *tanka* are identical in form to what today is known as haiku. This is no coincidence. While we normally think of the tradition of haiku as beginning with the great Edo-period poet Matsuo Bashō (1644–94), the tradition of writing verses in this form in fact goes back much further. Throughout its history the 5-7-5

---

1. Heian is one of the major divisions of Japanese history. During this period political power was located at the imperial court in Kyoto, giving rise to a sophisticated literary and artistic culture.

form has been characterized by a tension between the serious and light-hearted, and between the high and the low. We know, for example, that Heian period courtiers enjoyed a light-hearted poetic game known as *kusari renga* ('chained verses'). The game involved one person composing the first three 5-7-5 lines of a *tanka*, while someone else attempted to complete the poem by adding the following 7-7. The next person in the chain would then add another 5-7-5, and the game would continue for an indeterminate number of links. From quite early on, the first verse in this game, known as the *hokku*, was accorded a special respect: it needed to be a complete thought in itself, and convention dictated that it should be composed by the most accomplished poet at the gathering.

By the fourteenth century, this aristocratic party piece developed into a more serious art known simply as *renga*. A number of rules were drawn up to govern the permitted frequency of certain images, and the ways that one verse could be linked to the one that preceded it. *Renga* gatherings were a serious form of communal art that drew upon the participants' knowledge of classical literature and poetry. The best *renga* often have a pointedly nostalgic mood, as they look back on the refined aristocratic culture of the past.

In the sixteenth and particularly the seventeenth centuries, as increasing literacy rates and the development of printing created new audiences for cultural pursuits, a popular form of *renga* (*haikai no renga*) appeared. *Haikai no renga*, or simply *haikai*, was still a communally created form of art, but it was far freer in the kinds of vocabulary and imagery that were permitted, and it exploded in popularity in the expanding cities of Edo period (1603–1867) Japan. Different schools of *haikai* soon developed. Some like the Kyoto-based Teimon school stressed the importance of links to the older classical traditions, while others like the Osaka-based Danrin school put more of a premium on parody, head-spinning invention, and daring wordplay.

Bashō was the poet who did most to transform *haikai* from an energetic, often vulgar popular form back into something more serious. He maintained the free use of everyday imagery and accessible vernacular language, but created new depth by interrogating the relationship between man and nature, by finding parallels between the classical and the vernacular, and by focusing on lowly figures such as beggars, prostitutes and the elderly, who had rarely been the subjects of previous poetry. He developed the conventional form of haiku, including the inclusion of a seasonal word (*kigo*) and the linguistic 'cutting word' (*kireji*) that both split and joined the haiku into two sections.

Those poets that followed Bashō added their own elements to the form, though with many poets making a living through teaching, the temptation to codify innovations into strict rules gradually destroyed the spontaneity and freshness that haiku had originally been known for. A major attack on these stultifying conventions of the form was mounted in the late nineteenth century by a young poet called Masaoka Shiki (1867–1902). Shiki retained the seventeen-syllable form and the seasonal word, but he rejected all of the other rules. To distinguish this new, radical conception from what had come before, he suggested the term haiku. Shiki's innovations provided the foundations for a revitalization of haiku in the twentieth century. Its potential has expanded in multiple directions, incorporating virtually the full range of possible literary approaches – free verse, imagist, symbolist, surrealist.

Senryū

If Bashō and his followers represented the serious, high-culture side of haiku, there were other poets who saw its potential for observational humour – sometimes gentle, other times irreverent, black or maliciously cutting. In the late 1750s, a ward headman in the shogunal capital of Edo called Karai Senryū (1718–90) started to run public *maekuzuke* poetry contests. He published two seven-syllable lines, known as the *maeku*, and invited entrants to the competition to submit the three lines that would follow it (*tsukeku*). His contests began to attract more and more entries, till by the mid 1760s over 20,000 people were entering each time – each one paying a small entry fee. So popular were they that they began to be published in annual volumes, under the title *Yanagidaru* (*The Willow Barrel*) from 1765. While Senryū himself preferred to call these verses *maeku*, gradually his name became associated with the genre as a whole.

Senryū differ from haiku in that there is no requirement to use a seasonal or a cutting word. The focus is rather on human society, in all its earthiness and grotesqueness. Without the focus on nature and the contrastive structural dynamic of haiku, *senryū* were often little more than amusing puns or riddles. A contemporary essayist called Ogawa Akimichi (1737–1815/16) aptly described the nature of *senryū* as follows, 'playful verse that comments on human behaviours, virtues and vices, noble and base emotions, thoughts of upper and lower-class people, and all the other matters that make up this life on earth' (Ueda 1999, p. 20). As a genre *senryū* was unashamedly popular, though occasionally some intellectuals would compose it too. The lack of rules and openness of the subject matter meant some *senryū* were frankly bawdy or obscene. In time these more risqué *senryū* became known as *bareku*. *Senryū* has continued on into the twenty-first century, though it is a far less popular genre than haiku. But as haiku has become more colloquial and some *senryū* poets have experimented with less humorous verses, the boundary between the two forms has become less distinct.

Love

While love was one of the most popular topics in *tanka*, the haiku tradition has always placed a primary emphasis on depictions of nature. However, many haiku poets touched upon the topic, sometimes obliquely, sometimes more directly. The haiku and *senryū* collected here span several centuries: from the Edo period, then Japan's years of modernization in the late nineteenth and early twentieth century, and finally from the post-war period. Over the course of these three and a half centuries, the social expectations placed on women and men changed enormously. In the Edo period, women's conduct was rigorously policed both under the law and through moral education, and most marriages were arranged by parents and go-betweens. The major cities all contained large licensed quarters containing thousands of prostitutes. It was normal for men to choose a wife to manage his household and bear his children, and a mistress from the pleasure quarters for his love and pleasure. The discourse of Japan's years of modernization underlined the importance to the state of women being only 'good wives and wise mothers'. Which of course isn't to say that the human capacity and desire for romantic love was entirely stifled. We know that women in the Edo period enjoyed reading romantic *ninjōbon* novels, which were dismissively referred to as 'weeping books' due to the prevalence of hyper-emotional plots in which two women competed for the affection of a man. At the turn of the twentieth century, novels and plays that portrayed the conflict between pure love and money enjoyed huge audiences.

But what is perhaps most surprising about the human moments captured in haiku and *senryū* is just how resilient and recognizable are the emotions expressed. The clothes, the hairstyles, the domestic interiors may all be exotically different; the archetypal romantic figures might be the mythic Herdsman and Weaver Maiden, or the tragic Umegawa and Chūbei rather than Romeo and Juliet or Tristan and Iseult, but the emotional reality of those moments of revelation, and the capacity of the human heart to long for, to desire, to miss, to grieve is truly universal. The figures in parody are just as easily recognizable – the henpecked husband, the flighty bride, the foolish old man. The blushing embarrassment of a bride on the morning following her wedding, the jealousy inspired by a mistress or a woman from the licensed quarters, the mystery and joy of pregnancy, or the sudden awareness of the death of a spouse felt when encountering one of their possessions – each of these is immediately understandable, no matter what culture we have been brought up in.

The arrangement of poems in this book has borrowed a device from *tanka* poetry, which often arranged its chapters on love so that they charted the course of a courtly love affair from the first stirrings of longing, through the initial approaches and meetings, usually ending up in desertion and heartbreak. But since the haiku and *senryū* chosen cover all the stages of life, they have been arranged in three sections: one for the excitement of young love and passion, one for the negotiations and occasional disappointments of love in maturity, and a final section that depicts the consolations and losses that come to any relationship in old age.

so varied
and ever-changing—
love

Bonchō

さまざまに
品かはりたる
恋をして

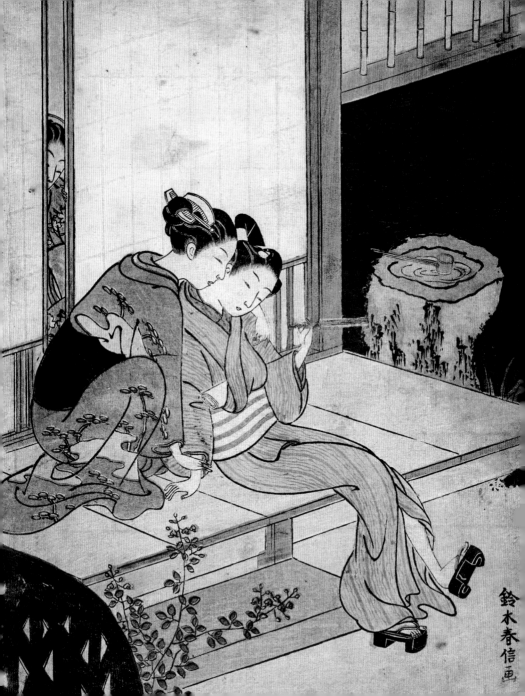

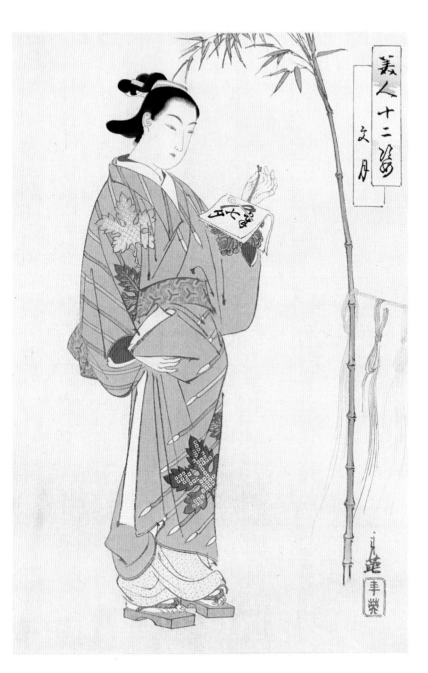

love's many forms —
all the threads of desire
begin in purest white

Buson

恋
さ
ま
ざ
ま

願
の
糸
も

白
き
よ
り

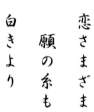

Migita Toshihide (1863–1925), *Seventh Month*
(*Fuzuki*), from the series *Twelve Figures of Beauties*
(*Bijin jūni sugata*), a set of twelve prints, one for each
month. Colour woodblock print, 19th century. 37 ×
25 cm. British Museum 1906,1220,0.1519.

the travelling players
made the village headman's daughter
lovesick

Anon.

旅芝居
庄屋の娘
ぶらつかせ

even while chopping
the dried vegetables for rice
her heart elsewhere

Yaba

上をきの
千葉刻むも
うはの空

Ogata Gekkō (1859–1920), girl kneeling in front of a
print of an actor, from the series *Women's Fashions
Collection* (*Fujin fūzoku tsukushi*). Colour woodblock
print, 1891. 36.8 × 25.4 cm. British Museum
1906,1220,0.1738.

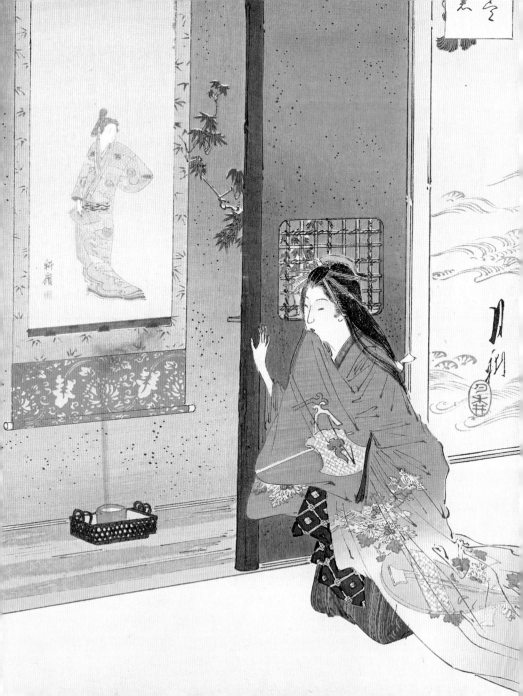

the girl
stares only at her fan
saying nothing

Gyūji Ichirō

団扇ばかり
見て娘
返事せず

longing for him,
I draw eyebrows on a melon
on the veranda

Sonome

人見んと
瓜に眉かく
端居かな

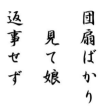

Kitagawa Utamaro (1753–1806), *The Courtesan
Morokoshi of the Echizenya*, from the series *Great
Beauties of the Current Day Collection* (*Tōji zensei
bijin-zoroi*). Colour woodblock print, undated. 38.1 ×
25.1 cm. British Museum 1922,0719,0.3. Bequeathed
by Charles Hazelwood Shannon.

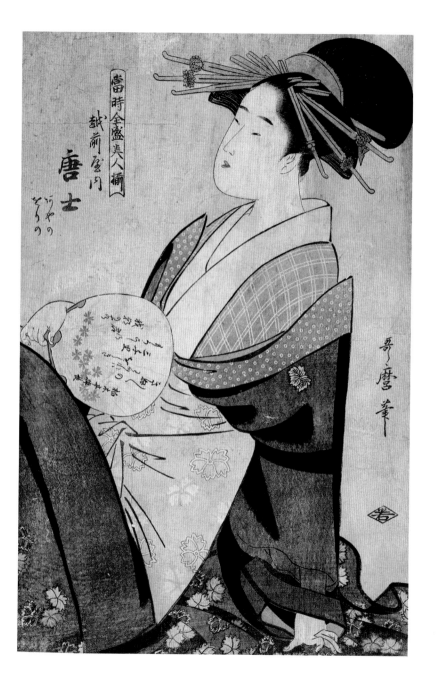

over my shoulder
I saw her under her umbrella
just a glance

Nishiyama Sōin

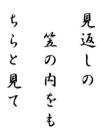

見返しの
笠の内をも
ちらと見て

so pleasing to my eye
the fan of my beloved—
purest white

Buson

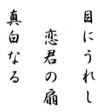

真白なる
恋君の扇
目にうれし

Teisai Hokuba (1771–1844), geisha on landing
stage in snow. Hanging scroll; ink, colour and gold
on silk, 1830–44. 102.9 × 14.4 cm. British Museum
1980,0630,0.5.

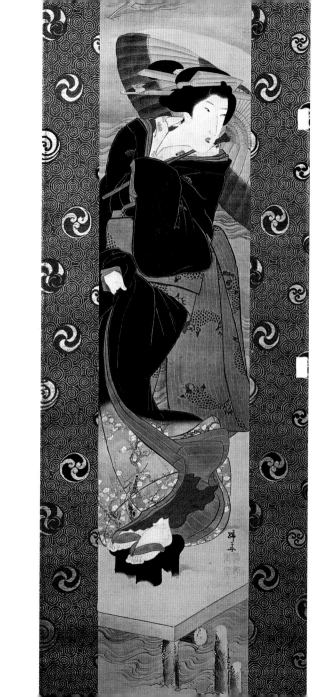

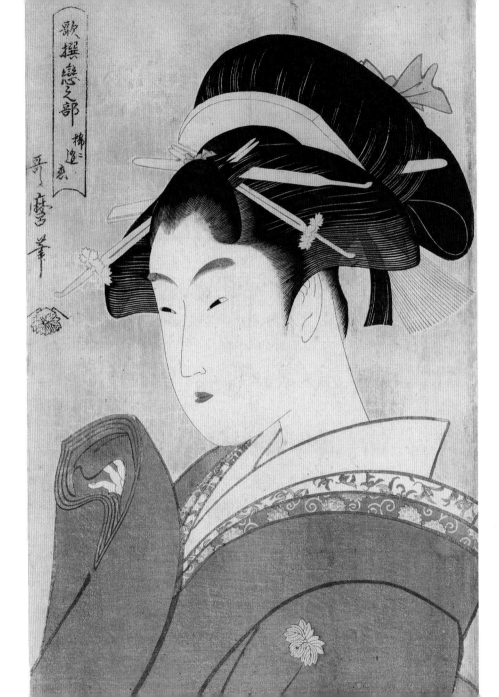

the love letter
from a man she despises —
she shows it to mother

Anon.

わがすかぬ
男のふみは
母に見せ

Kitagawa Utamaro (1753–1806), *Love that Rarely Meets* (*Mare ni au koi*), from the series *Anthology of Poems: The Love Section* (*Kasen koi no bu*). Colour woodblock print, *c.*1793–4. 38.3 × 25.1 cm. British Museum 1906,1220,0.331.

combing
my hair, love-struck,
sparks scatter

Matsuda Kyōmi

恋
の
髪

梳
き
て
火
の
粉
を

ふ
り
こ
ぼ
す

a shooting star —
in love, not knowing
where it will lead

Mayuzumi Madoka

流
星
や

行
方
知
れ
ず
の

恋
を
し
て

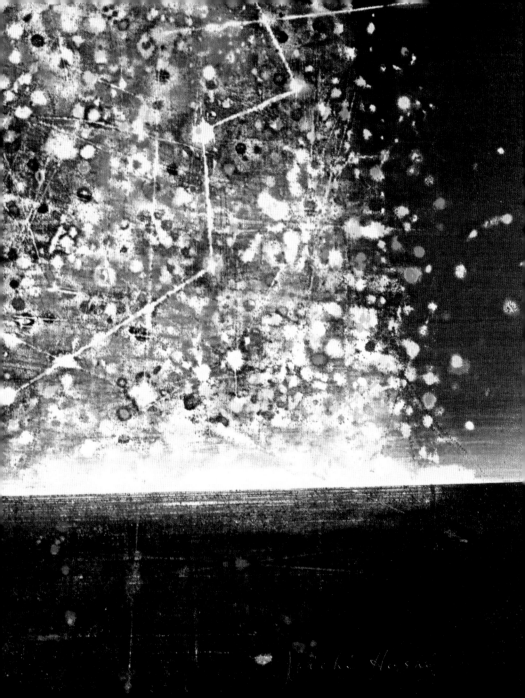

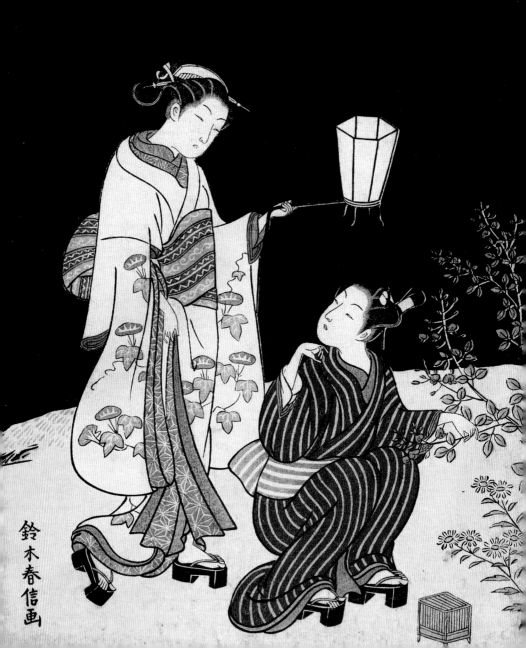

holding hands
under a moon bright enough
to make us feel shy

Yoshino

つなぐ手の
はづかしい程
月が冴え

first love —
drawing close to a lantern
two faces

Taigi

初恋や
灯籠に寄する
顔と顔

beneath the moon
insects play
a symphony of love

Wafū

月の下
虫らが恋の
シンフォニ

by the sparkler
she grasps, my darling's arm
illuminated

Yamaguchi Seishi

手花火に
妹がかひなの
照さるる

Kobayashi Kiyochika (1847–1915), *Fireflies at Ochanomizu (Ochanomizu Hotaru)*. Colour woodblock print, 1880. 24.5 × 36.3 cm. British Museum 1943,0508,0.5.

spring rain—
in our palanquin, you whisper
sweet nothings

Buson

春雨や
同車の君が
さゝめごと

umbrella-sharing—
the one more in love
gets wet

Keisanjin

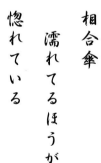

相合傘
濡れてるほうが
惚れている

Kitagawa Utamaro (1753–1806), *The Courtesan Umegawa and the Courier Chūbei* (*Keisei Umegawa, Hikyakuya Chubei*), from the series *True Feelings Compared: The Founts of Love* (*Jitsu kurabe iro no minakami*). Colour woodblock print, *c*.1800. 38.6 × 25 cm. British Museum 1924,0115,0.25.

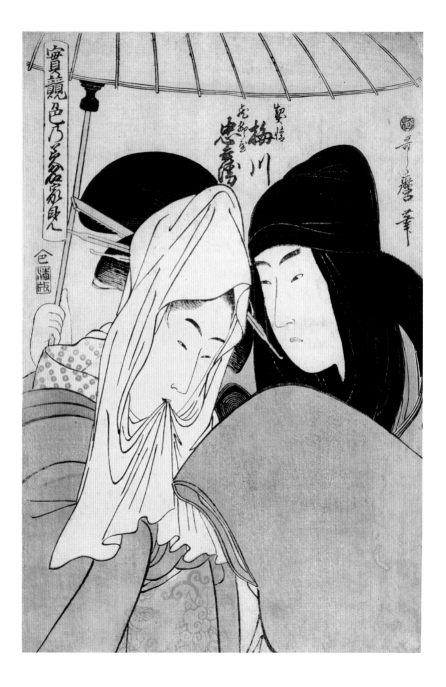

moonflowers —
when a woman's skin
glows white

Chiyo-ni

夕顔や
女子の肌の
見ゆる時

hearing footsteps
and splitting into two —
a shadow

Anon.

影法師
二つにわれる
足音で

Yokoyama Kazan (1781–1837), husband and wife
seated on straw matting beneath moonflowers.
Hanging scroll; ink and colours on silk, *c.*1800–37.
87.5 × 31 cm. British Museum 1881,1210,0.2724.

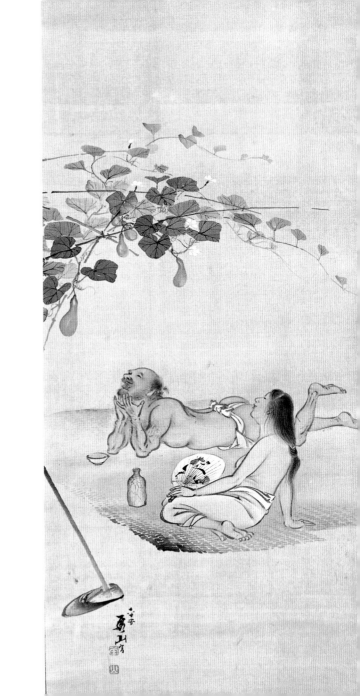

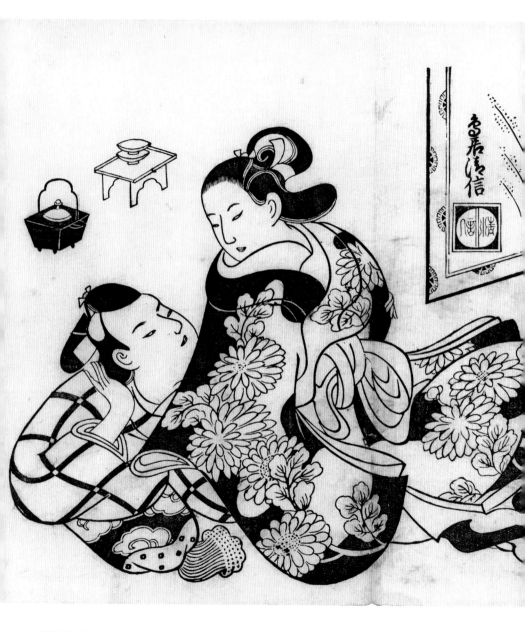

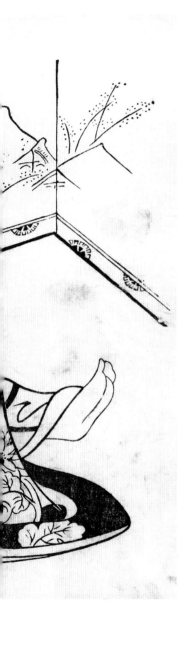

onto his silent lap
she lowers her
eloquent hips

Anon.

口きかぬ
膝へ口きく
膝をのせ

Torii Kiyonobu (1664–1729), a courtesan and her client, from a set of seven *shunga* prints. Woodblock print, 1704–11. 22.7 × 33.2 cm. British Museum OA+,0.65.

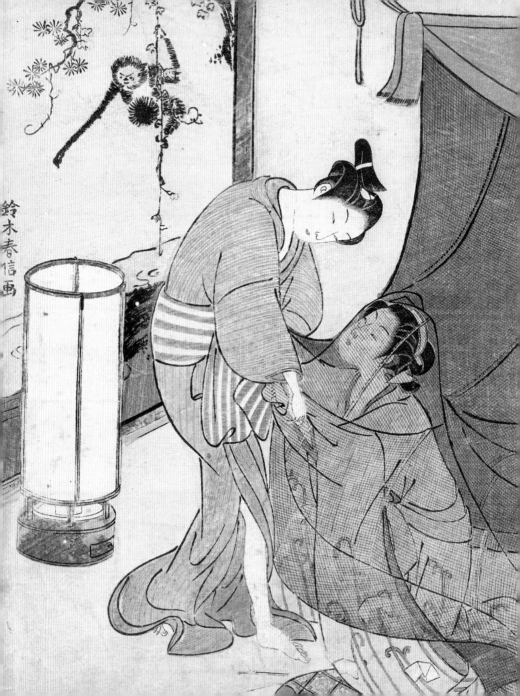

to snuff out
the candle, she borrows
the man's breath

Anon.

ろうそくを
消すに男の
息をかり

don't, please…
when she whispers it
you're halfway there

Anon.

よしなあの
低いは少し
出来かかり

Suzuki Harunobu (1725–70), girl under a mosquito net
with her lover. Colour woodblock print, undated. 26.7 ×
19.5 cm. British Museum 1937,0710,0.45. Bequeathed
by Charles Hazelwood Shannon.

teased by
every visitor—the bride
the morning after

Anon.

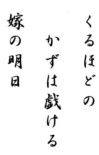

くるほどの
かずは戯ける
嫁の明日

Utagawa Kuniyoshi (1797–1861), women preparing for
a wedding ceremony. Central panel from a woodblock
triptych print, undated. 36 × 25 cm. British Museum
2008,3037.20304. On loan from Prof. Arthur R. Miller.

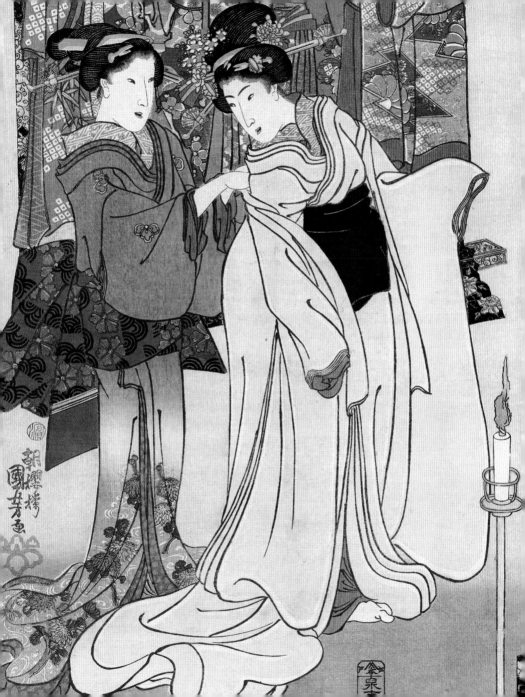

finally wed,
his face became
human

Anon.

女房を
もつて人相
面になり

what's both
valuable and tiresome?
a wife

Anon.

重宝な
物で邪魔なは
女房なり

Toshusai Sharaku (*fl.* 1794–95), the kabuki actor
Onoe Matsusuke as the impoverished samurai
Matsushita Mikinoshin in the kabuki play *Katakiuchi
Noriaibanashi.* Colour woodblock print, 1794–5.
36.2 × 24.6 cm. British Museum 1909,0618,0.42.

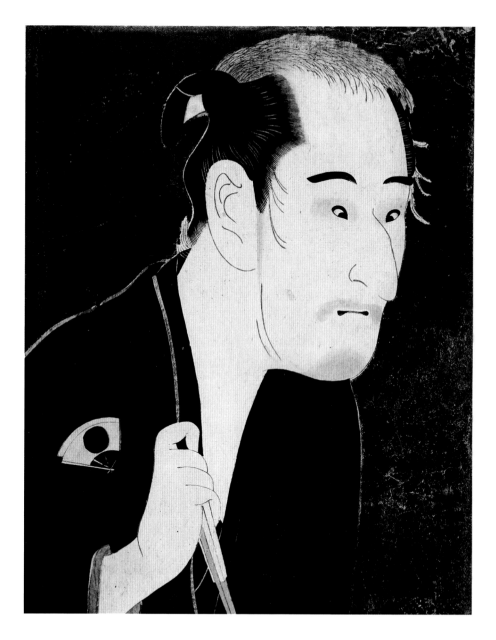

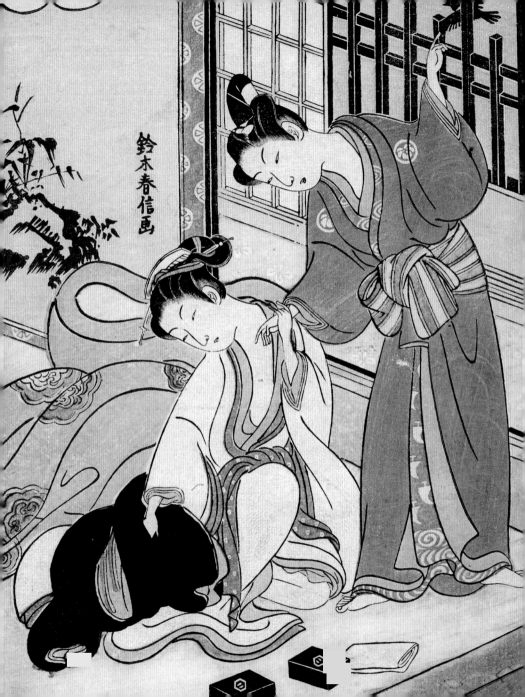

weeping
and wailing – the husband
gives in

Anon.

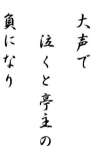

Suzuki Harunobu (1725–1770), lovers parting
sorrowfully. Colour woodblock print, 1765–70.
27.4 × 20.4 cm. British Museum 1906,1220,0.66.

quarrel abates—
the one who looks in the mirror
is the woman
Anon.

仲直り
鏡を見るは
女なり

reconciliation—
his wife's voice
returns to normal

Anon.

仲直り
元の女房の
声になり

Utagawa Kunisada (1786–1864), lady inserting
a comb into her hair in a mirror, from the series
Contemporary Make-up Mirrors (*Imafū keshō kagami*).
Colour woodblock print, 1823. 37.2 × 25.7 cm.
British Museum 1915,0823,0.878.

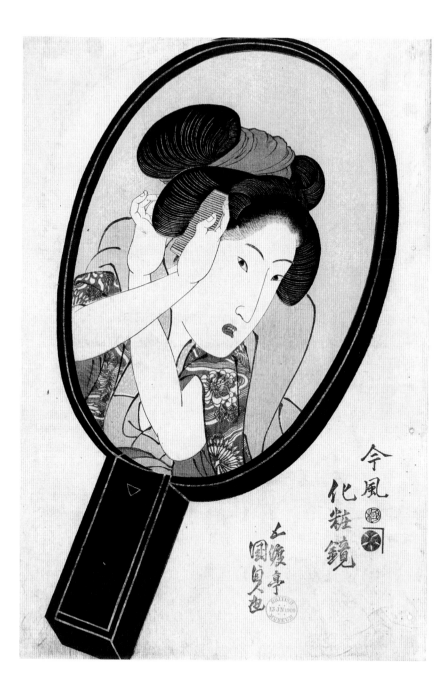

今風
化粧鏡

女渡亭
國貞画也

first hands,
then their feet touch—
an armistice

Anon.

手がさわり
足がさわって
仲直り

burning mosquitos
in the concubine's bedchamber—
erotic whispers

Kikaku

蚊をやくや
褒㜷が閨の
私語

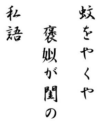

Kitagawa Utamaro (1753–1806), from *Poem of the
Pillow* (*Utamakura*). Colour woodblock print, 1788.
25.5 × 37 cm. British Museum OA+,0.133.6.

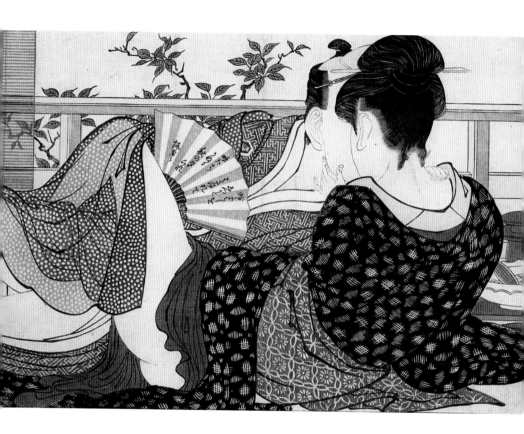

one's own wife
in the daylight, delicious
as stolen love

Anon.

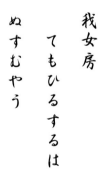

我女房
てもひるするは
ぬすむやう

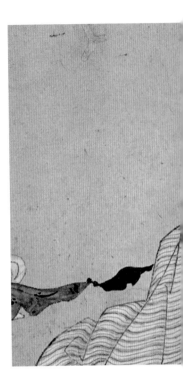

Attributed to Katsukawa Shun'ei (1762–1819).
Untitled *shunga*, one of ten scenes of lovemaking.
Detail of a handscroll; ink, colour and mica on paper,
1792–95. Overall: 27.9 × 638.1 cm. British Museum
1980,0325,0.4.

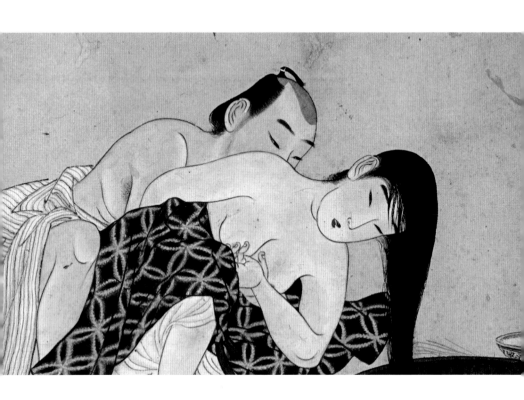

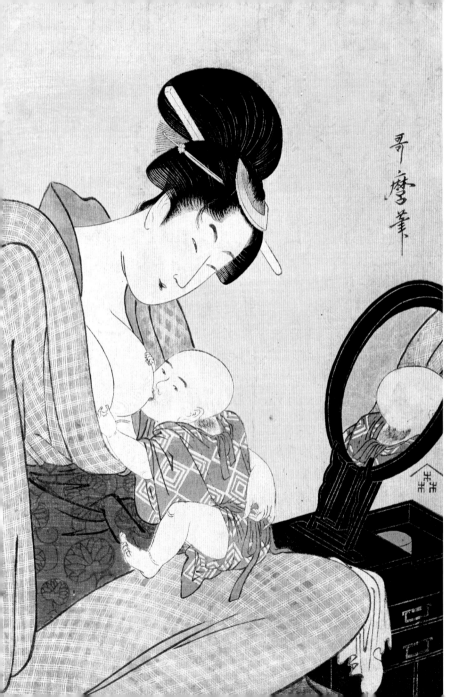

the Milky Way—
since my wife became pregnant
it seems even whiter

Takaha Shugyō

天の川
妊りてより
天白さ増す

since the birth
bossing him around
has become a habit

Anon.

産あげく
夫使うが
癖になり

Kitagawa Utamaro (1753–1806), a mother suckling
her baby in front of a toilet mirror. Colour woodblock
print, late 1790s. 38.4 × 26.1 cm. British Museum
1937,0710,0.99. Bequeathed by Charles Hazelwood
Shannon.

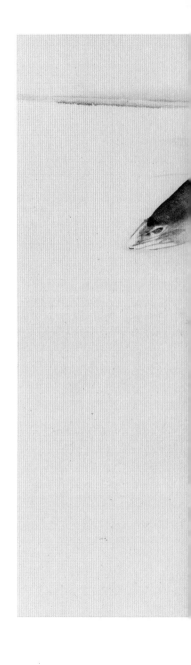

suckling the baby
she says, "there's sardines
on the shelf"

Anon.

添え乳して
棚にいわしが
ござりやす

Shibata Zeshin (1807–91), fish. Colour woodblock
print, undated. 29.1 × 44 cm. British Museum
1906,1220,0.1367.

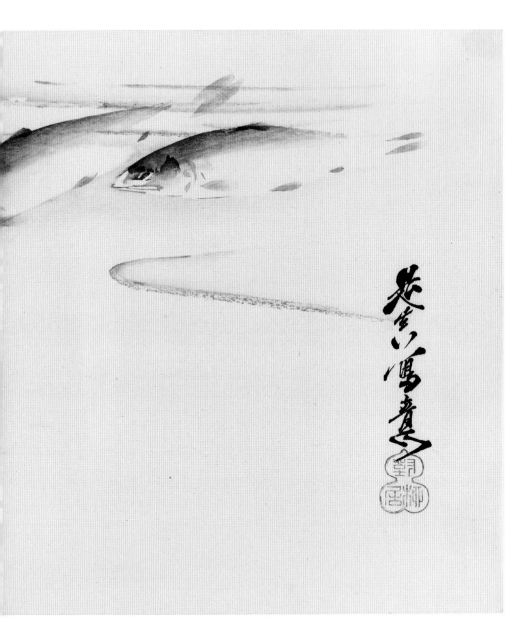

a bat swoops past—
the wife from across the street
glances my way

Buson

かはほりや
むかひの女房
こちを見る

the young wife's
dreams scamper across
the corridor

Anon.

新造の
夢は廊下を
かけ廻り

Hosoda Eishi (1756–1829), woman dreaming
of *The Tales of Ise.* Hanging scroll; ink, colour
and gold on silk, 1795–1818. 88.7 × 31.2 cm.
British Museum 1913,0501,0.407. Bequeathed
by Sir William Gwynne-Evans, Bt.

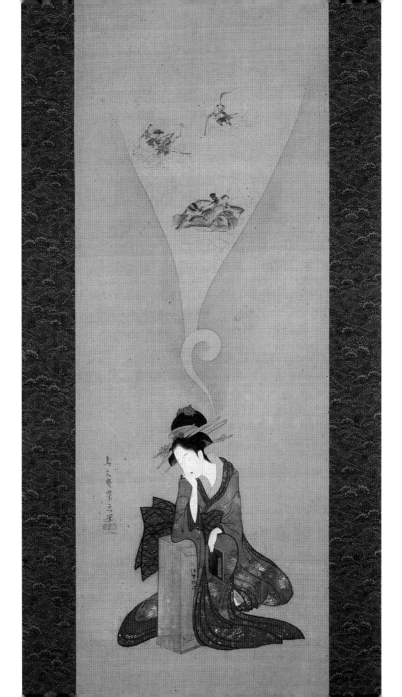

the wife counts
the nights
he slept at home

Anon.

家に寝た
夜を女房に
数えられ

Attributed to Katsukawa Shun'ei (1762–1819).
Untitled *shunga*, one of ten scenes of lovemaking.
Detail of a handscroll; ink, colour and mica on paper,
1792–95. Overall: 27.9 × 638.1 cm. British Museum
1980,0325,0.4.

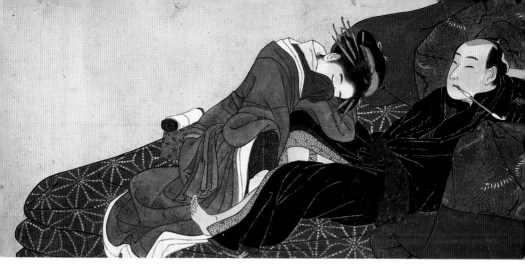

choosing a swimsuit
when did I start seeing
through his eyes?

Mayuzumi Madoka

水着選ぶ
いつしか彼の
眼となつて

blossoms in full bloom:
a debauched priest and
a fickle wife

Bashō

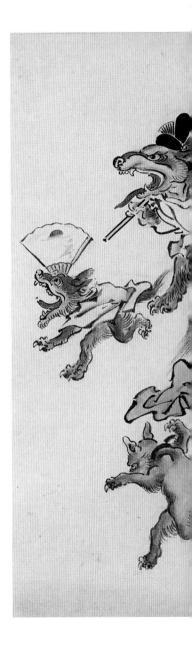

盛りぢや花に
坐浮法師
ぬめり妻

Kawanabe Kyōsai (1831–89), demon women and
dancing cats. Sketch; ink and colours on paper, 1879.
38.1 × 52.7 cm. British Museum 1881,1210,0.1836.

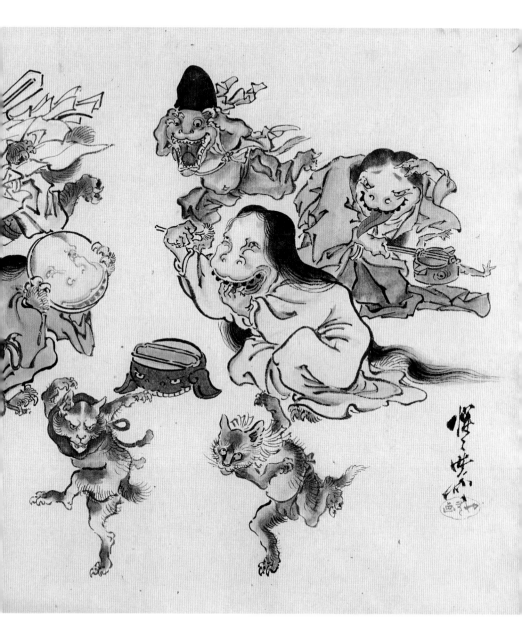

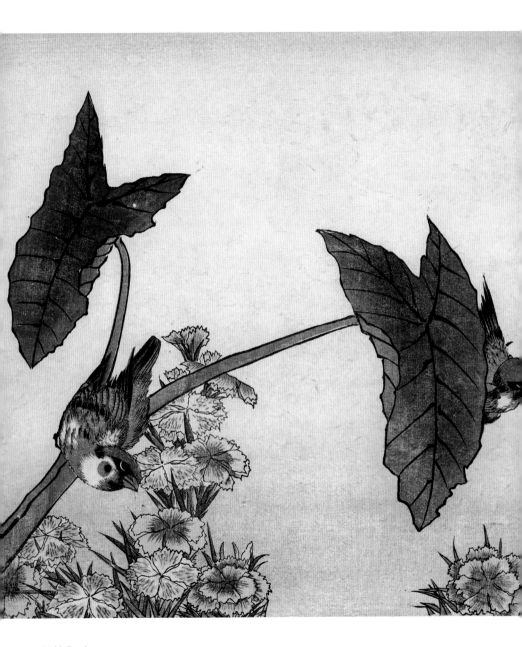

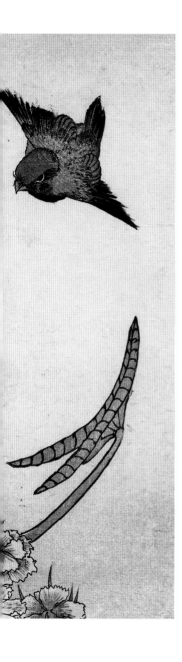

why?
as she sips on her gruel
eyes brimming

Anon.

なに故ぞ
粥すするにも
涙ぐみ

moss pinks
planted by the husband,
trampled by his wife

Kamakura Sayumi

芝ざくら
夫が植えて
妻が踏む

After Katsushika Hokusai (1760–1849), pinks and
leaves with sparrows. Colour woodblock print,
c. late 19th century. 25.1 × 36.8 cm. British Museum
1937,0710,0.226. Bequeathed by Charles Hazelwood
Shannon.

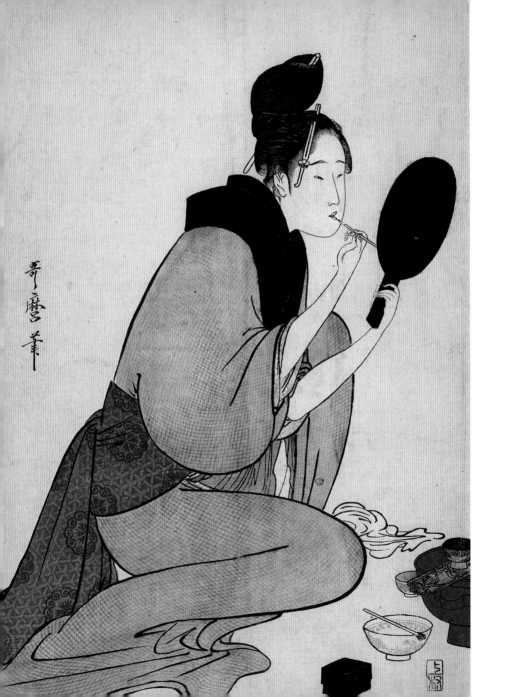

stifling yawns
stifling myself
I remain wife

Matsuda Kyōmi

欠伸を殺し
わたしを殺し
妻でいる

Christmas—
this sadness of being a wife
when did I first feel it?

Katsura Nobuko

クリスマス
妻のかなしみ
いつしか持ち

Kitagawa Utamaro (1754–1806), girl applying make-
up to her mouth. Colour woodblock print, undated.
37.7 × 25.1 cm. British Museum 1920,0514,0.6.
Bequeathed by R. N. Shaw.

undesired
wife, her bones pale
purple

Tokizane Shinko

抱かれざる
妻のうすむら
さきの骨

love leaving
passes
love coming in

Anon.

でる恋に
うちへくる恋
すれちがい

Tsukioka Yoshitoshi (1839–92), *Ishiyama Moon* (*Ishiyama
no tsuki*) from the series *One Hundred Aspects of the
Moon* (*Tsuki hyaku sugata*). Colour woodblock print,
1889. 37 × 24.9 cm. British Museum 1906,1220,0.1415.

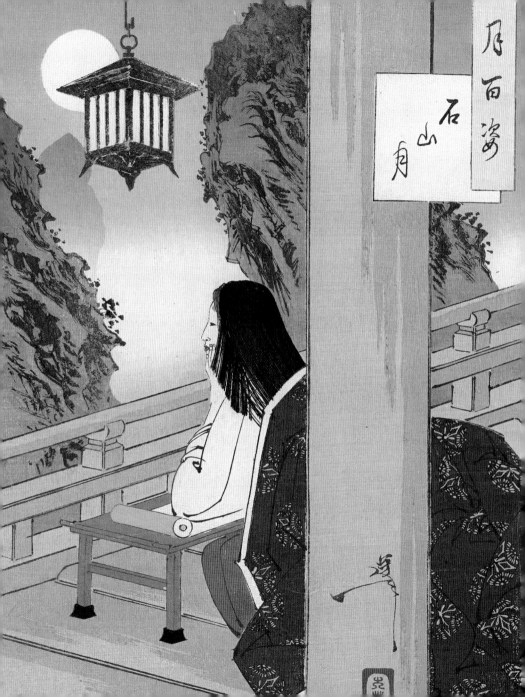

plucking his lice
a beggar's wife
under a plum tree

Buson

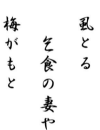

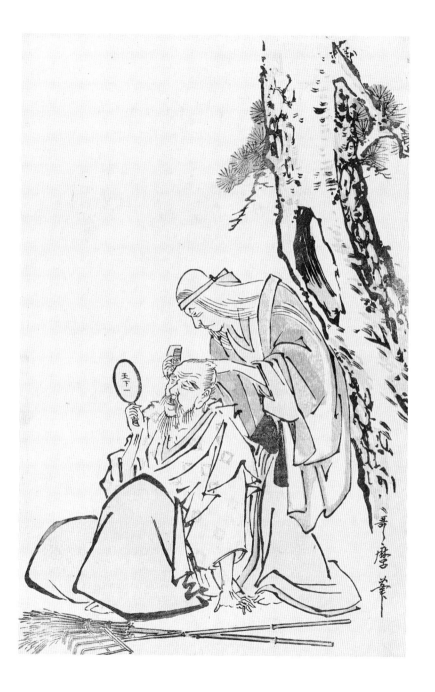

no secrets
left to hide, my wife
has grown old

Anon.

隠す事
なくて女房の
老いにけり

with few words
husband and wife part—
autumn nightfall

Sugita Hisajo

言葉少く
別れし夫婦
秋の宵

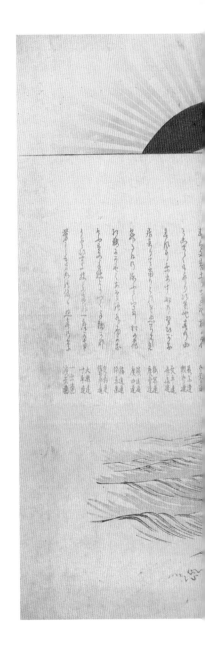

Kawakami Gyokuen (active mid 19th century), the
old couple of Takasago, seated beneath a pine tree.
Colour woodblock print, 1851–75. 29 × 53.4 cm.
British Museum 1902,0212,0.412.

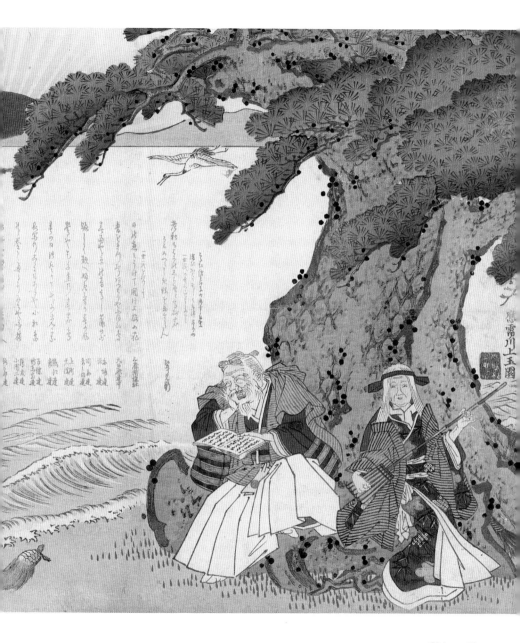

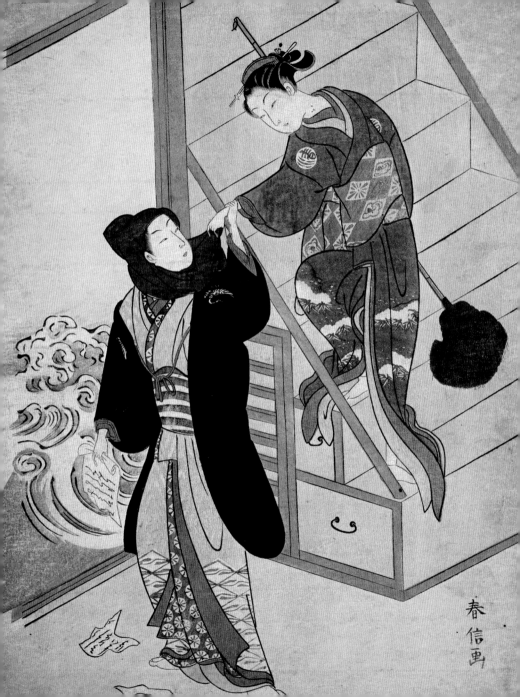

no lust
no love
just domestic cares

Anon.

恋もなし
外に色気も
世体苦の

fifty-year-old bridegroom
hiding his head
under a fan

Issa

五十婿
天窓を隠す
扇かな

Suzuki Harunobu (1725–70), girl with mop, trying to
prevent her lover leaving. Colour woodblock print,
undated. 28.3 × 21 cm. British Museum 1937,0710,0.26.
Bequeathed by Charles Hazelwood Shannon.

sleeping, waking
the emptiness
of my mosquito net

Chiyo-ni

起きてみつ
寝てみつ蚊帳の
広さかな

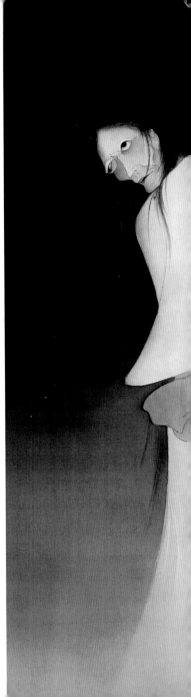

Takayama Umpo (dates unknown), female ghost tying
up mosquito net. Hanging scroll; ink, colour and gold
on silk, early 20th century. 115.4 × 46.8 cm. British
Museum 2002,1218,0.1.

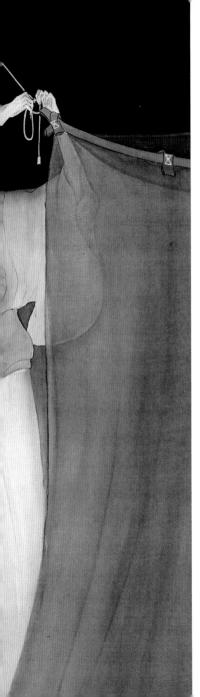

in bed alone
I hear a male mosquito
buzzing sadly

Chigetsu

独り寝や
夜わたる男蚊の
聲侘し

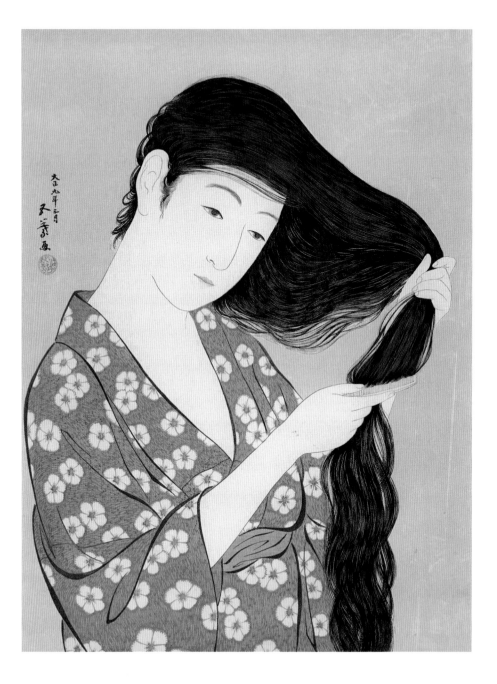

a sudden chill—
treading on my dead wife's comb
in our bedroom

Buson

身にしむや
亡妻の櫛を
閨に踏

Hashiguchi Goyo (1880–1921), *Combing the Hair* (*Kamisuki*). Colour woodblock print, 1920. 44.8 × 34.8 cm. British Museum 1930,0910,0.1.

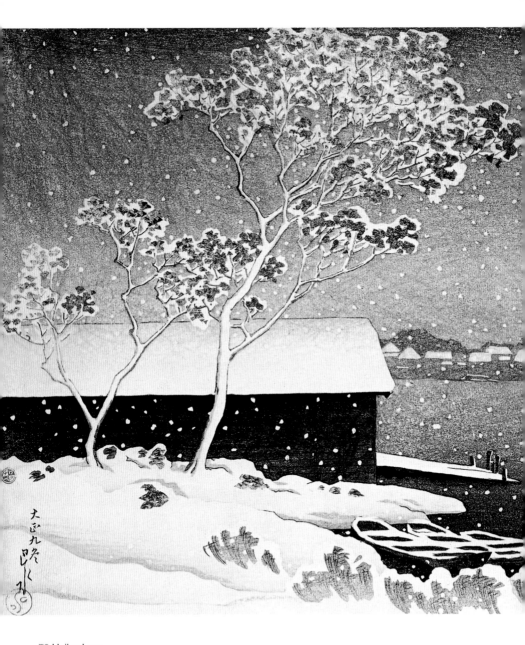

76 Haiku: Love

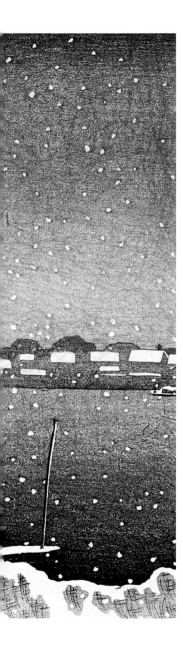

my husband gone—
from the bluest of skies
spring snow falls

Takeshita Shizunojo

つま行くと
晴天春の
雪をふる

don't cry, insects!
lovers must always part
even the stars

Issa

鳴な虫
別るる恋は
ほしにさへ

Kawase Hasui (1883–1957), *Shirahige in the
Snow* (*Yuki no Shirahige*), from the series *Twelve
Tokyo Subjects* (*Tokyo jūnidai*). Colour woodblock
print, 1920. 27.1 × 38.9 cm. British Museum
1946,0209,0.69. Bequeathed by Arthur Morrison.

at daybreak
speaking to the blossoms
a woman all alone

Enomoto Seifu

あかつきの
花にものいふ
一人哉

falling blossoms —
even now, I can't believe
she's dead

Saikaku

ちる花や
今に死んだと
思はれず

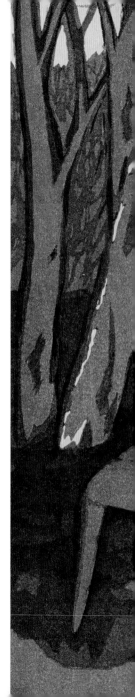

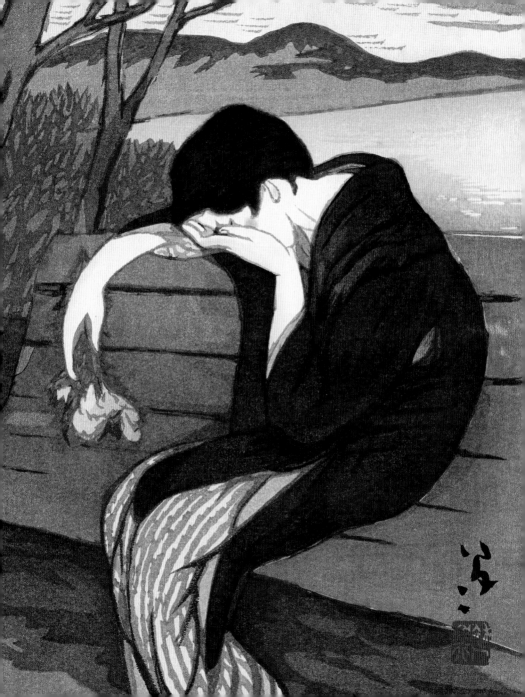

only a dream—
how cold the empty half
of an old man's bed

Nishiyama Sōin

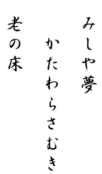

みしや夢
かたわらさむき
老の床

Utagawa Toyokuni I (1769–1825), portrait of the
publisher Eijudō on his 71st birthday. Colour woodblock
print, 1797–98. 37.7 × 25.1 cm. British Museum
1921,0216,0.3.

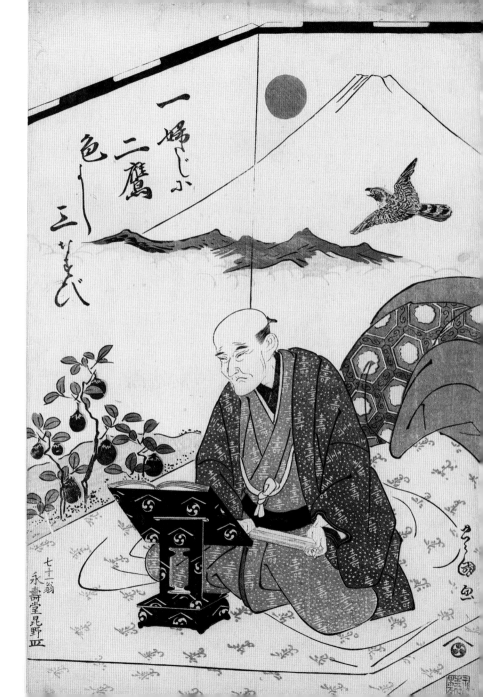

closing my eyes
I luxuriate in the warmth
of loves long past

Hino Sōjō

眼をとぢて
むかしの恋に
あたたまる

if only she were
still here to complain to —
tonight's moon

Issa

小言いふ
相手もあらば
今日の月

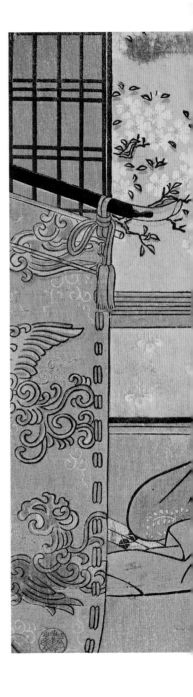

Suzuki Harunobu (1725–70), lovers embracing behind
a screen. Colour woodblock print, undated. 19.3 ×
23.2 cm. British Museum 1937,0710,0.43. Bequeathed
by Charles Hazelwood Shannon.

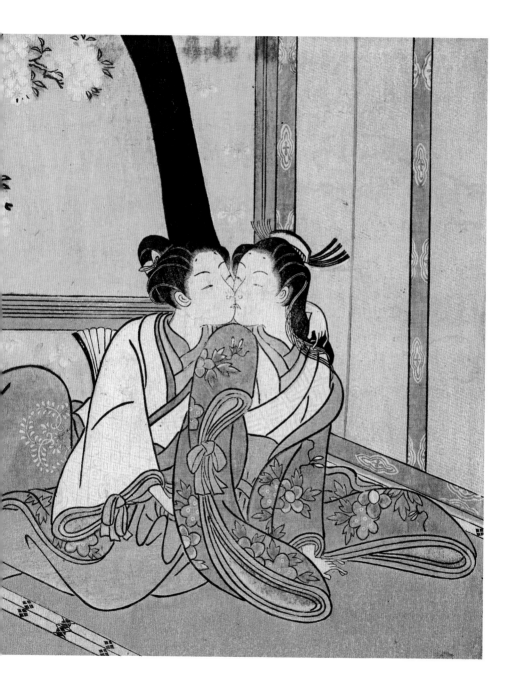

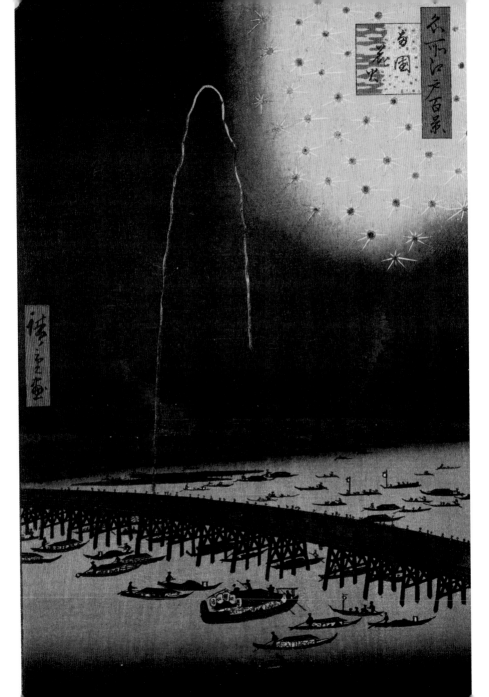

love is smoke —
stardust-like,
but smoke nonetheless

Kamakura Sayumi

恋
は
け
む
り

星
屑
に
似
て

い
る
け
む
り

Utagawa Hiroshige (1797–1858), *Fireworks at Ryogoku*, number 98 in the series *One Hundred Views of Edo* (*Meisho Edo Hyakkei*). Colour woodblock print, 1858. 35.5 × 24.1 cm. British Museum 1906,1220,0.746.

wifeless, I said
so the landlord gave me
a maiden flower

Yamamoto Kakei

妻
な
し
と

家
主
や
く
れ
し

女
郎
花

old man's love
whenever I try to forget
late autumn rain

Buson

老
が
恋

わ
す
れ
ん
と
す
れ
ば

し
ぐ
れ
か
な

Utagawa Hiroshige (1797–
1858), woman standing in
front of clumps of cotton
rose and courtesan flower.
Hanging scroll; ink and colour
on silk, 1837–44. 36.5 ×
55.3 cm. British Museum
1946,0209,0.44. Bequeathed
by Arthur Morrison.

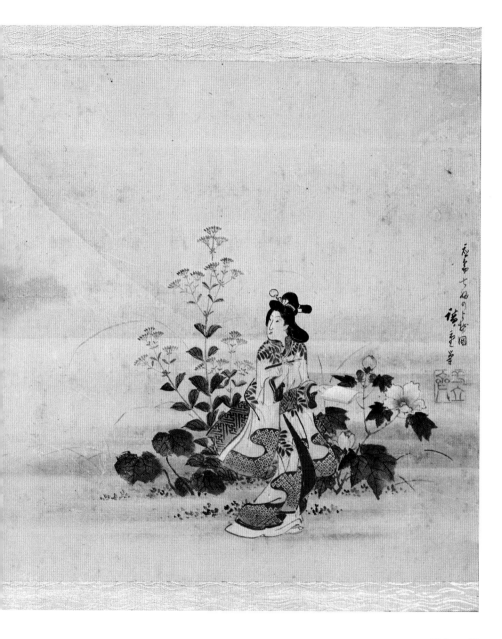

see how they love!
if I am reborn, let me be
a butterfly in the field

Issa

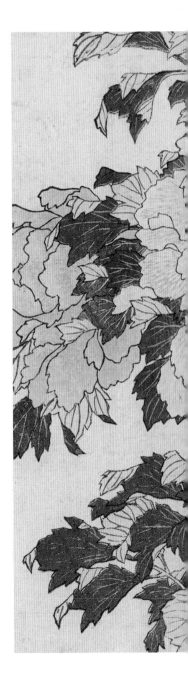

むつましや
生まれ変はらば
野辺の蝶

Katsushika Hokusai (1760–1849), flowers, peonies and butterfly (detail). Colour woodblock print, 1830s. 24.5 × 36.4 cm. British Museum 1926,0112,0.2.

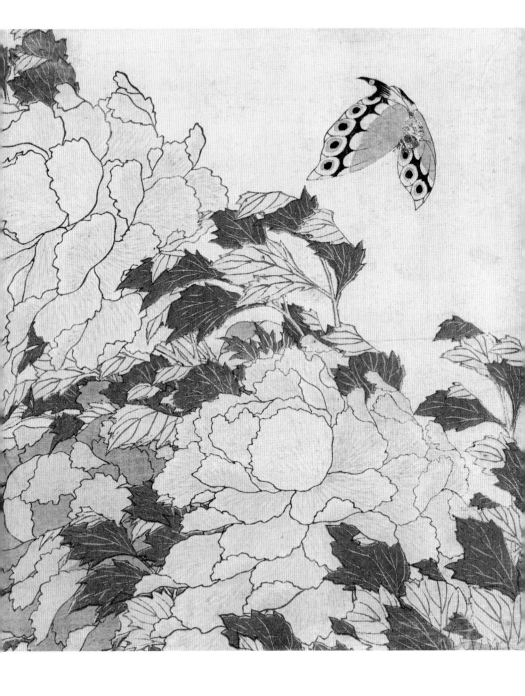

Biographical notes

Names have been given in the normal Japanese order, with the family name first, followed by the given name or poetic pseudonym. Many poets are known by a pseudonym (*haigō* or *haimyō*). Thus, Matsuo Bashō is referred to as Bashō, his *haimyō*, and not by his family name, Matsuo. There is very little biographical data for many Tokugawa period (1603–1867) *senryū* poets, as their poems were submitted to contests anonymously and published under their pseudonyms. As a result, it has not been possible to find biographical data on Gyūji Ichirō, Keisanjin, Wafū or Yoshino.

Matsuo BASHŌ (1644–94). The most significant poet in the development of *haikai* as a literary genre. Bashō was born in the castle town of Ueno, thirty miles south-east of Kyoto. His family were originally members of the samurai class, but by the time of Bashō's birth had become farmers. He studied *haikai* from a young age, first writing Teimon school-style verses, then later after he moved to Edo in 1672, coming under the influence of Nishiyama SŌIN. After several years as a commercial *haikai* master in the city, in 1680 he moved to Fukagawa, just outside the city and began to develop his own style of recluse poetry. The last years of his life were occupied by numerous journeys across Japan, during which he composed with local poets as well as visiting famous poetic sites. Bashō's greatest achievement was to create a new poetics of everyday life, accessible yet refined and profound, with a sharp observational sensitivity. The poetic style he developed, known as the *shōfū* (Bashō-style), is still practised by thousands of poets in Japan.

Nozawa BONCHŌ (1640?–1714). Born in Kanazawa, he moved to Kyoto where he practised as a doctor. He became a disciple of BASHŌ, and edited *The Monkey's Straw Raincoat* (*Sarumino*), an anthology of poems by Bashō and his students. His best poems are marked by their objectivity and lucidity.

Yosa BUSON (1716–83). Born in current day Hyogo prefecture, Buson first studied in Edo with the poet Hajin (1676–1742), then in the north-east of Japan, before moving to Kyoto. He was a noted painter as well as a poet, exemplifying the Chinese-influenced *literati* (*bunjin*) ideals of the latter half of the eighteenth century. His verse is immensely flexible, marked by storytelling and portraiture, and the creation of playful, imaginative worlds. *See* Makoto Ueda, *The Path of Flowering Thorn: The Life and Poetry of Yosa Buson* (Stanford: Stanford University Press, 1988); and Cheryl A. Crowley, *Haikai Poet Yosa Buson and the Bashō Revival* (Leiden: Brill, 2007).

Kawai CHIGETSU (c.1634–1718). Born in Kyoto. A female poet and member of Bashō's school. She was particularly close to BASHŌ and hosted him at her house in Ōmi on several occasions. For more translations of her haiku, see Makoto Ueda, *Far Beyond the Field*, (New York: Columbia University Press, 2003).

Fukuda CHIYO-NI (1703–75). Also known as Chiyo-jo. The most famous and prolific female haiku poet in Tokugawa Japan, Chiyo-ni was born in Kanazawa into a family that specialized in the mounting of pictures on scrolls and screens. Her poetry closely followed the Bashō-style, with a clear and unadorned focus on natural topics. Her reputation fell considerably in the twentieth century following criticism by the poet Takahama Kyoshi (1874–1959). *See* Patricia Donegan and Yoshie Ishibashi. *Chiyo-ni: Woman Haiku Master* (Tokyo: Charles E. Tuttle, 1996).

Sugita HISAJO (1890–1946). Born in Kyushu as the daughter of a government official, she spent her early years in Okinawa and then Taiwan. She studied haiku under Takahama Kyoshi (1874–1959), and started a haiku magazine for female

poets, *Hanagoromo,* in 1932. Famously, she was expelled from Kyoshi's circle in 1936 for reasons still unknown. Her life has been frequently dramatized into novels, plays, and several television series.

Kobayashi ISSA (1762–1827). Born into a middle-class farming family in Nagano, he lost his mother at an early age. When his father remarried, Issa left home at age 14 and moved to Edo where he first started studying haiku and took the *haimyō* Issa ('Cup of Tea'). His later life was marked by a series of tragedies –a bitter inheritance dispute with his stepmother, the deaths of his children and wife, and his house burning down. His poetry is highly unorthodox, with a liberal use of dialect, humour, and a focus on insect and animal imagery. *See The Spring of my Life and Selected Haiku,* translated by Sam Hamill, (Boston: Shambhala, 1997).

Yamamoto KAKEI (1648–1716). Kakei was a doctor in Nagoya, and he became an early disciple of BASHŌ. However, he was more conservative than other members of Bashō's circle and was highly critical of new developments in their style. Eventually he became estranged

from the circle, and in his later years he abandoned haiku altogether, becoming a teacher of the older style of linked verse (*renga*).

Enomoto KIKAKU (1661–1707). Born as the eldest son of a doctor in Edo, he became one of the first and best of Bashō's students. After his teacher's death, he opened his own haiku school in Edo. Said to have been fond of drink, his haiku often exhibits a gaudy, dramatic sense of wit and style.

Matsuda KYŌMI (1942–). Female *senryū* poet from Kyushu.

Mayuzumi MADOKA (1962–). One-time TV reporter, now one of the best-known contemporary female haiku poets. Mayuzumi is noted for her use of stylish urban imagery – sunglasses, Porsches, mannequins, etc. She has published seven volumes of verse, as well as several volumes of essays, translations, and travel journals. For more translations of her haiku, see Makoto Ueda, *Far Beyond the Field* (Columbia University Press, New York, 2003), or in French, *Haikus du temps present*, translated by Corinne Atlan (Paris: Philippe Picquier, 2012).

Katsura NOBUKO (1914–2004). Published her first verses in *Kikan*, a haiku magazine founded by Hino SŌJŌ. Her style changed quite radically over the course of her career, from the erotic physicality of her early works to the simpler emotionalism of her later years.

Ihara SAIKAKU (1642–93). Born into a well-to-do merchant family in Osaka, Saikaku is best known today as a novelist. His dazzling, witty stories captured all the life of the licensed quarters and mercantile districts of the bustling cities of Tokugawa Japan. However, he began his writing career as a *haikai* (linked verse) poet, specializing in the earthy humour, colloquial language, and wordplay of the Danrin school. *See* Christopher Drake, 'The Collision of Traditions in Saikaku's Haikai', *Harvard Journal of Asiatic Studies*, Vol. 52, No.1 (June 1992).

Kamakura SAYUMI (1953–). She started writing haiku while at university and has published six volumes of her own verse. She is editor of the haiku magazine *Ginyu* and treasurer of the World Haiku Association. Married to the haiku poet Natsuishi Ban'ya. *See A Crown of Roses*, translated by James Shea and James Kacian (Cyberwit.net, 2009).

Enomoto SEIFU (1732–1815). Born into a samurai family, Seifu was probably initiated into the writing of haiku by her stepmother. She studied under two teachers: Shirai Chōsui (1701–69) and Kaya Shirao (1738–91). Her verse displayed a rare sense of colour and drama. While little praised during her lifetime, Seifu's verse was rediscovered during the early twentieth century and now enjoys a high reputation.

Yamaguchi SEISHI (1901–94). Born in Kyoto and began writing haiku while at high school. After being introduced by Hino SŌJŌ, a friend from Kyoto University, he began studying with Takahama Kyoshi (1874–1959) in 1922. He later became a leading light in the New Haiku movement, which was radical in its use of urban imagery and was suppressed in the early 1940s. Seishi's post-war poems focused on the oppositions between humanity and nature as he returned to a more BASHŌ-influenced style.

Tokizane SHINKO (1929–2007). Born in Okayama, she started submitting *senryū* to newspapers in her mid-twenties. Her first collection of poetry was self-published in 1963; its free-spirited sensuality and emotional depth was compared to the early twentieth century *tanka* poet, Yosano Akiko (1878–1942). A 1987 collection *Yūfuren* became a bestseller, and she became a well-known *senryū* commentator in the media.

Takeshita SHIZUNOJO (1887–1951). Born in a rural community in Kyushu, she worked as a schoolteacher and, following her husband's early death, as a librarian. She was a member of Takahama Kyoshi's *Hototogisu* (*Mountain Cuckoo*) haiku circle. Her poetry often drew upon images of life in impoverished rural Kyushu.

Takaha SHUGYŌ (1930–). Born in Yamagata. He began writing poetry while at high school, and in the late 1940s he studied with Yamaguchi SEISHI. His first collection of verse was published in 1965, and he has gone on to publish several dozen books and win many literary prizes. His verse frequently depicts contemporary society, with a distinctive dry lyricism.

Nishiyama SŌIN (1605–82). Born into a samurai family in Kumamoto, Sōin later studied linked verse (*renga*) in Kyoto, before becoming one of the founders of the *haikai* movement. While living in Osaka, he founded the iconoclastic Danrin-style of *haikai*, which stressed spontaneity, unbridled invention and freedom, in form, subject, and language. Ihara SAIKAKU was Sōin's best known student.

Hino SŌJŌ (1901–56). Born in Tokyo, he spent his childhood in Korea, before entering Kyoto University. While still at high school he started a student haiku circle, which published its own magazine. In 1929 he became a member of the haiku group of the most famous poet of the early twentieth century, Takahama Kyoshi (1874–1959), however, he would be expelled following the publication of the suggestively erotic 'Miyako Hotel' series of verses in 1934. Later in his life, his poetry moved away from its early experimentalism towards a more tranquil, traditional style.

Shiba SONOME (1664–1726). Born near the Grand Shrine of Ise, it is thought that she began writing haiku from an early age. Her husband, an eye doctor called Shibai Ichiyū, shared her interest in poetry, and the two of them welcomed BASHŌ to their home in 1688. She later moved to Osaka, where she continued to write poetry and judge haiku contests. Following her husband's death, she moved to Edo where she compiled two anthologies of haiku.

Tan TAIGI (1709–71). A gifted and eccentric poet, who spent much of his life as a wanderer between different places and different haiku styles. Famously he lived for a time in the Shimabara licensed quarter of Kyoto under the patronage of a brothel keeper, setting up a haiku studio where he took students. He was a leading member of the Bashō Revival movement of the latter half of the eighteenth century, and enjoyed a close relationship with BUSON.

Shida YABA (1662–1740). A clerk at a money exchange business in Edo. He first studied with KIKAKU, then later with BASHŌ. As a central member of Bashō's circle, he acted as editor for the *Sack of Charcoal* (*Sumidawara*) collection. After his master's death, he moved to Osaka where he was said to have over one thousand students.

Further reading

Addiss, Stephen, 2012, *The Art of Haiku: Its History through Poems and Paintings by Japanese Masters* (Boston & London: Shambhala).

Blyth, Reginald H., 1949–52, *Haiku*, 4 vols (Tokyo: Hokuseidō Press). 1961, *Edo Satirical Verse Anthologies* (Tokyo: Hokuseidō Press).

Carter, Stephen D., 1991, *Traditional Japanese Poetry: An Anthology* (Stanford: Stanford University Press).
2011, *Haiku Before Haiku – From the Renga Masters to Bashō* (New York: Columbia University Press).

Donegan, Patricia and Yoshie Ishibashi, eds and trans., 1996, *Chiyo-ni: Woman Haiku Master* (Tokyo: Charles E. Tuttle).

Gill, Robin D., 2007, *The Woman Without a Hole & Other Risky Themes from Old Japanese Poems* (Florida: Paraverse Press).

Kobayashi Issa, 1997, *The Spring of my Life and Selected Haiku*, translated from Japanese by Sam Hamill (Boston: Shambhala).

Mayuzumi Madoka, 2012, *Haikus du temps présent*. Translated from Japanese by Corinne Atlan (Paris: Philippe Picquier).

Sato, Hiroaki, 2008, *Japanese Women Poets: An Anthology* (Armonk & London: M.E. Sharpe).

Shirane, Haruo, 1998, *Traces of Dreams: Landscape, Cultural Memory, and the Poetry of Bashō* (Stanford: Stanford University Press).

Ueda, Makoto, 1982, *Matsuo Bashō: The Master Haiku Poet* (Tokyo: Kōdansha International).
1988, *The Path of Flowering Thorn: The Life and Poetry of Yosa Buson* (Stanford: Stanford University Press).
1999, *Light Verse from the Floating World: An Anthology of Premodern Japanese Senryū* (New York: Columbia University Press).
2003, *Far Beyond the Field* (New York: Columbia University Press).

Sources of translations

All of the haiku reproduced in this book have been newly translated by the author, with the exception of the following:

pp. 35 and 64, Anon.

From *Haiku: An Anthology of Japanese Poems*, translated by Stephen Addiss, Fumiko Yamamoto, and Akira Yamamoto, © 2009 by Stephen Addiss, Fumiko Yamamoto, and Akira Yamamoto. Reprinted by arrangement with The Permissions Company, Inc., on behalf of Shambhala Publications Inc., Boston, MA. www.shambhala.com.

p. 48, Anon.

From *The Woman Without a Hole & Other Risky Themes from Old Japanese Poems,* translated by Robin D. Gill (Florida: Paraverse Press, 2007), p. 422. © Robin D. Gill

Credits